Chickerella was thrilled to see
all the gowns at the Fowl Ball.

"Sky blue pink is my favorite color," cried Chickerella. "It's beautiful!"

"Yeah, I'm good. Coulda made a fortune as a fashion designer."

"Now I remember the story!" Chickerella exclaimed. "You'll turn a pumpkin into a coach."

"I don't do transportation, dearie. I'll call a cab, but at midnight the cabbie goes off duty and the snazzy outfit goes *poof*!"

The prince was charmed by the eggsquisite stranger and danced every dance with her, even though they couldn't carry on a conversation over Penny Pullet and the Rock Island Reds' music.

"Fairy Goosemother, I'd love to go to the Fowl Ball."

"So, go already. Although why you want to is beyond me. The band is Penny Pullet and the Rock Island Reds. They sound like chicken toenails on broken eggshells."

"But I have nothing to wear. If I had some silk and a few beads I'd make a gown."

"I'll speed things up." The Fairy Goosemother waved her wand.

When the band finally took a break, Chickerella heard the clock strike midnight. "I must go!" she cried.

As she dashed out the door, she felt an egg coming on. "I can't stop to lay an egg!"

But there's no holding back an egg that's on its way, especially a slippery glass one. Chickerella ran headlong down the castle steps.

She was too late! The cab drove away. Then the gown disappeared in a burst of fireworks, and Chickerella ran cluck naked all the way home.

The next day, Chickerella heard a commotion. "Hear ye! Hear ye! The prince seeks the mysterious hen he met at the Fowl Ball. The only clue she left is this egg. All single hens, please present your eggs."

"Look, mine have big yolks," said Cholestera.

"She *is* a big yolk," said Ovumelda.

"The egg must match the one in this velvet bag," said the prince. "Does anyone else live here?"

The stepmother blocked the prince's view. "No, Your Highness."

"I live here!" cried Chickerella.

But the prince didn't hear her. He and the page turned to leave.

"Wait! I lay *glass* eggs! Is that what you're looking for?"

"That's eggsactly what I'm looking for! Release her at once."

"Your Highness surely wouldn't marry my servant, Chickerella."

"Finding a bride was my mother's idea," said the prince. "I only went to the ball to see all the fancy gowns."

"Oh, me too!" exclaimed Chickerella, running out into the sunlight.

"Your costume was eggcellent, my dear."

"Thanks, Your Highness. I'm really into fashion."

There was a burst of sparkles. "Fashion? Did I hear fashion?"

"I'm into eggscessories," said the prince. "Especially shoes."

"We all love clothes," said Chickerella. "Let's start our own fashion business."

"Done!" declared the prince. "We'll name it after you."

So the Fairy Goosemother zapped up some fabulous fabrics, Chickerella cut and stitched, and the prince designed stylish shoes to match. That's how they started the fashion line called Chickerella.

Their first show in New Yolk was an
eggstravaganza.

Chickerella had a wonderful chickhood until one night when a fox got into the coop and carried off her mother. Chickerella's father, now a single rooster, did his best to raise her, providing her with a happy and stable cooplife.

Then a few years later a hen from another farm showed up with her two daughters and convinced Chickerella's father to marry her. Chickerella was eggscited to have a new family.

Chickerella

by **Mary Jane** and **Herm Auch**

Holiday House / New York

This book is dedicated to our daughter, Katrin,
who generously sacrificed her junior prom dress to be cut apart
and remade into Chickerella's sky blue pink ball gown.

Notes on the art for this book

Mary Jane created the stuffed chicken mannequins and wired them so they were posable. She formed the heads with polymer clay, then covered them with chicken feathers. Each character had a variety of eyes and beaks to change the facial expressions. She knitted the wings from shaggy yarns. She designed and made all of the outfits. The shoes were sculpted from polymer clay. Buckles and crowns were formed with copper or silver wire and "jewels."

Herm created the sets from a mixture of found and constructed objects of varying sizes. He made a miniature photo studio with movable lights. He then photographed all of the elements separately, with the lighting and point of view needed for each scene. He combined them in the computer, scaling everything to the appropriate size and adding special effects.

Chickerella's glass egg was created by glass sculptor Milon Townsend.

Text copyright © 2005 by Mary Jane Auch
Illustrations copyright © 2005 by Mary Jane and Herm Auch
All Rights Reserved
Printed in the United States of America
www.holidayhouse.com
3 5 7 9 10 8 6 4 2

Library of Congress Cataloging-in-Publication Data
Auch, Mary Jane.
Chickerella/ by Mary Jane Auch; illustrated by Mary Jane and Herm Auch.—1st ed.
p. cm.
Summary: This barnyard version of the Cinderella story features a mild-mannered chicken,
a fashion-conscious Fairy Goosemother, and a prince at a Fowl Ball.
ISBN 0-8234-1804-9 (hardcover)
ISBN 0-8234-2015-9 (paperback)
[1. Fairy tales. 2. Chickens—Fiction.] I. Auch, Herm, ill. II. Title.
PZ8.A9234Ch 2004
[E]—dc21
2003047864

ISBN-13: 978-0-8234-1804-6 (hardcover)   ISBN-10: 0-8234-1804-9 (hardcover)
ISBN-13: 978-0-8234-2015-5 (paperback)   ISBN-10: 0-8234-2015-9 (paperback)

She even put her sewing skills to use, making three dresses as welcome gifts for her stepmother and new stepsisters, Ovumelda and Cholestera.

"Such a sweet girl," said the stepmother with a smile that gave Chickerella hen bumps.

Before long, the stepmother sent Chickerella's father off on a wild goose chase. Then she proceeded to redecorate.

"This doesn't look like home anymore," Chickerella said.

"That's because it's *my* coop now, not yours," said the stepmother. "You have too many clothes. I want you to let out your dresses to fit my girls."

"But what will *I* wear?" asked Chickerella.

"You're just a servant now. You only need one dress and you won't be living in the main coop anymore."

From then on, the stepmother locked Chickerella in the springhouse every night.

Chickerella's days were filled with work. She prepared all the meals but wasn't allowed to eat with her stepfamily.

She ate the bugs that clung to the springhouse walls and drank the crystal clear water that bubbled up through its floor.

After a short time on this odd diet, Chickerella noticed that the shells of her eggs were becoming more and more transparent, until soon she was laying eggs of pure glass.

One day the stepsisters came home all aflutter. "The prince is seeking a bride," said Ovumelda.

"He's invited every unmarried hen to the Fowl Ball," added Cholestera.

"I've always wanted to go to a ball," said Chickerella.

"Don't be silly," said the stepmother. "The prince would never marry a servant."

"Who wants to get married?" Chickerella asked. "I just want to see the fancy ball gowns."

"Out of the question," answered the stepmother. "Now start making my daughters look beautiful. We don't have much time."

Chickerella's next few days were filled with frantic preparations.
Making the stepsisters presentable wasn't easy, especially when they
kept adding their own eggasperating touches to their outfits.
When the big night arrived . . .

. . . the stepmother locked Chickerella in the springhouse. Later, as Chickerella was dozing off, the springhouse fizzed with sparkles.

"Yikes! Who are you?" gasped Chickerella.

"What, you've never read a fairy tale? I'm your Fairy Goosemother. I've been watching your stepmother run you ragged. Why doncha speak up?"

"My father will fix everything when he gets back."

"Don't wait for someone else to fix things, dearie. You take charge. Fantastic eggs, though. How do you do that?"

"I think it's something in the water."

"Oh yeah. I put a spell on this spring a while back. Cool side effect."

And together the three friends worked happily ever after.